INDY RACE CARS

MOTOR Mania

by Janet Piehl

Jan Lahtonen, consultant and safety engineer, auto mechanic, and lifelong motor sports enthusiast

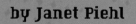 Lerner Publications Company • Minneapolis

Special thanks to Lisa Teyema and her family

For Jeffrey and the Motor Mania Club

Cover Photo: Tomas Scheckter leads the 2005 IndyCar® Series Peak Antifreeze Indy® 300 at Chicagoland Speedway in Joliet, Illinois.

Indy® is a registered trademark of Brickyard Trademarks, Inc.

Lerner Publications Company
A division of Lerner Publishing Group
241 First Avenue North
Minneapolis, MN 55401 U.S.A.

Website address: www.lernerbooks.com

Library of Congress Cataloging-in-Publication Data

Piehl, Janet.
    Indy race cars / by Janet Piehl.
      p.   cm. — (Motor mania)
    Includes bibliographical references and index.
    ISBN-13: 978–0–8225–6566–6 (lib. bdg. : alk. paper)
    ISBN-10: 0–8225–6566–8 (lib. bdg. : alk. paper)
    1. Indy cars—Juvenile literature. I. Title.
TL236.P5275 2007
796.72—dc22   2006019394

Manufactured in the United States of America
1 2 3 4 5 6 – DP – 12 11 10 09 08 07

Contents

Introduction—What Is an Indy Race Car?   4

Chapter One—Indy Race Car History   6

Chapter Two—Indy Racing Culture   22

Indy Race Car Gallery   34

Glossary   46

Selected Bibliography   46

Further Reading   46

Websites   46

Index   47

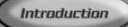
WHAT IS AN INDY RACE CAR?

Airplanes streak across the Indiana skies. Marching bands play patriotic songs. Colorful balloons float above the track. Excited fans of all ages jam the stands.

What's all the fuss about? It's the Greatest Spectacle in Racing, the Indianapolis, or Indy, 500. As many as 350,000 fans are ready for auto racing's most important day.

Indy style race cars compete in the Indianapolis 500. This famous 500-mile (805-kilometer) race takes place every Memorial Day weekend in the town of Speedway, near Indianapolis, Indiana. It is the largest-attended, single-day sporting event in the world.

The Indy 500® is by far the best-known Indy car race. But the cars also compete in other races in the Indy Racing League® (IRL) IndyCar® Series. Most of the races take place in the United States. But the IRL also races in Japan.

Indy cars don't look like vehicles that drive on the street. They are sleek, high tech, compact, and low to the ground. Most importantly, Indy cars move fast. They zoom around racetracks at speeds of up to 230 miles (370 km) per hour. At speeds that fast, the drivers face danger and chase glory. And they do it all in front of roaring crowds.

The 33-car field lines up at the starting grid of the Indianapolis Motor Speedway just moments before the Indianapolis 500 race begins.

Chapter One

INDY RACE CAR HISTORY

Marco Andretti sits in the cockpit of his number 26 Andretti Green Racing team car.

Indy cars are a kind of open-wheel race car. That means the cars' wheels do not have fenders. The cars have open cockpits. Drivers have no roof over their heads. The cockpit is part of a strong, narrow tub called a monocoque. The monocoque is part of the chassis, the main part of the car. All the other parts of the car are connected to the chassis. The engine sits in the back of the chassis, behind the cockpit. The suspension connects the wheels to the car.

Smooth and slim, Indy cars are aerodynamic. They are shaped so that air flows over them easily. For example, the outside shell of a car, called the bodywork, is smooth and carefully

Dan Wheldon pilots his number 10 Target Chip Ganassi Racing car at the Infineon Raceway in 2006.

rounded. The cars also have wings on the front and back. The wings work to create downforce. As the car moves forward, air pushes the wings down, pressing the car firmly onto the track. The wings help the car to speed through turns without tipping over or sliding off the track.

The Beginnings

Indy cars haven't always been so quick and sleek. Early cars had open wheels and open cockpits. But not much else was the same.

The first automobiles were developed in the late 1800s. By 1894 people were holding auto races throughout Europe and in the United States. The events were a huge hit with the public. People enjoyed watching the curious new vehicles racing on city streets and country roads. The noise and speed thrilled the crowds.

OPEN-WHEEL RACE CARS

Indy race cars are one of several different kinds of open-wheel race cars. Champ Cars, which race in the Champ Car World Series®, are another. Formula One cars, which compete in races around the world, are also open-wheel race cars.

Spectators line the sides of the Indianapolis Motor Speedway during the very first Indianapolis 500 race in 1911.

In time, people began to build tracks just for racing. Carl Fisher of Indiana was one such person. Fisher was the owner of a company that made headlights for cars. He wanted Indianapolis to be at the center of the fast-growing automobile industry. So Fisher and some business partners built the Indianapolis Motor Speedway in 1909. Fisher hoped it would be a popular place for automakers to test and race their cars. The oval track ran 2.5 miles (4 km). In 1911 Fisher decided to hold one 500-mile (805 km) race.

Fisher offered a prize of $10,000 (about $181,818 in 2000 dollars) to the winner of the first Indianapolis 500 International Sweepstakes. Any car that could travel at 75 miles (120 km)

per hour for a quarter mile (0.4 km) from a standing start could enter. Forty cars competed.

The winner, Ray Harroun, clocked an average race speed of 74.6 miles (120 km) per hour. It took him 6 hours and 42 minutes to finish. The race was a big success and became a yearly event. The long, high-stakes contest quickly gained importance. In the end, Detroit, Michigan, became the hub of the U.S. auto industry. But thanks to Carl Fisher and the Indy 500, Indianapolis is still famous for cars.

The Indy 500 joined other races. It became part of a series of races that made up the American Automobile Association (AAA) National Championship. With its huge crowd

WINNING WASP

Ray Harroun was not just the first winner of the Indianapolis 500. He is believed to be the first person to put a rearview mirror on a car. The mirror helped him watch out for the other cars in the race. Harroun drove a yellow and black car with a pointed yellow tail, which the press called the Wasp.

and big-money prize, the Indy 500 was the most important race in the series.

European cars led the pack at the Speedway for most of the 1910s. French automakers Peugeot and Delage won the race four times between them.

The cars of the time were very simple. The wheels, engine, and cockpit were all mounted to a strong, ladder-like frame. The engine sat near the front of the car. The cockpit was at the rear. The driver sat upright. His head and shoulders were above the cockpit.

The Indy 500 was canceled in 1917 and 1918 because of World War I (1914–1918). But things sped up again in 1919. Drivers from Europe and the United States battled for top spots. The cars got faster. That year, race winner Howdy Wilcox posted an average speed of 88 miles (142 km) per hour. American carmaker Duesenberg ruled the 1920s, winning four races. In 1925 Peter DePaolo became the first driver to win at an average speed of more than 100 miles (160 km) per hour.

During the 1930s, the United States was in the middle of the Great Depression. The U.S. economy was in tatters. Jobs were scarce, and many people were very poor. Most Americans couldn't afford new cars. Automakers struggled to stay in business. They could not spend money on making special race cars. Also, prize money was hard to come by. Still, drivers and spectators kept coming to the races.

In those days, deadly crashes were common. For instance, three drivers and two mechanics died during the month of the 1933 Indy 500. Speedway officials looked for more ways to cut down on accidents. They covered parts of the bumpy brick track with smooth asphalt. This new covering made it easier to control the cars. The turns were widened to give drivers more room for error.

Eddie Rickenbacker *(above)* had been a race car driver before becoming a fighter pilot in World War I. He owned the Speedway from 1927 to 1945. He made many safety improvements to the track, including paving over parts of the track's brick surface with asphalt. This photo of the starting grid for the 1923 race *(right)* shows the Speedway's old bricks. The surface earned the track the nickname the Brickyard.

Another Speedway safety improvement involved building a wall to separate the pit area from the track. This photo taken before the 1938 race shows how close the pit area was to the track.

Drivers such as Wilbur Shaw, Tommy Milton, and Louis Meyer enjoyed great success during this period. Shaw and Meyer each won the Indy 500 three times. Milton won it twice. Meanwhile, race speeds climbed. Better car designs and more powerful engines led to race speed averages of around 115 miles (185 km) per hour in the late 1930s.

World War II (1939–1945) shut down the Speedway—and all other auto racing—between 1942 and 1945. After the war, the neglected track was overgrown with weeds. Racing fan and Indiana businessman Anton "Tony" Hulman bought the track. He soon took the Indy 500 to new heights. In the years after World War II, huge crowds watched Mauri Rose and Bill Holland chase each other to victory. In 1949 Hulman offered the biggest prize yet. The winner would receive more than $50,000.

Anton "Tony" Hulman

The Hulman Years

The huge prize led some racers to design cars just for running—and winning—at Indianapolis. Race car builder Frank Kurtis earned fame for his new designs. Kurtis invented a race car that came to be known as a "roadster." His machines were shaped almost like tubes. They had long noses and were very low to the ground. This made them more aero-dynamic than the older, taller cars.

Kurtis experimented with setting the engine toward the left side of the car. This gave the car better balance. It shifted the car's weight to the inside of the track's left-hand turns. Kurtis also moved the cockpit to the right-hand side of the car. Without the engine directly in front of him, the driver had more legroom. He could sit lower in the car. Kurtis's cars won five out of six Indy 500s between 1950 and 1955. Popular driver Bill Vukovich won the 1953 and 1954 races. His average speed in 1954 was 130 miles (209 km) per hour.

In the mid-1950s, the United States Auto Club (USAC) took over running

Two-time Indy 500 winner Bill Vukovich poses in his Frank Kurtis-built roadster before the 1955 race. The popular driver was killed in a crash during the race.

Indy racing. It created rules for races and for the design of the cars. Drivers competed at Indy and in other races for the USAC Championship Car Series title.

In the early 1960s, Formula One drivers from Europe came to race in the United States. Stars such as Jim Clark and Graham Hill took on American greats A. J. Foyt, Parnelli Jones, Mario Andretti, and many others. The Formula One drivers brought cars that featured cutting-edge technology. In the 1963 Indy 500, Jim Clark drove a Lotus with a rear-mounted engine. Clark finished second in the race. Soon other teams began to build cars with rear-mounted engines. The rear-engine design allowed builders to lower the front section of the car. This made the car less bulky and more aerodynamic. Also, the cars had better balance. They were easier to handle. By 1969 the front engine was a thing of the past.

A. J. Foyt's pit crew springs into action during the 1961 Indy 500. The crew is changing the car's tires and refilling the fuel tank.

Many consider Mario Andretti *(in car)* to be the greatest American race car driver of all time. But he enjoyed little success at the Indy 500. In 29 races, he won just once—in 1969.

The 1960s also saw changes to the cars' chassis. The tube-shaped monocoque replaced the old ladderlike frame. The driver sat in the monocoque. The engine was attached to the back. Made of aluminum, the monocoque was very strong and lightweight. It provided good protection in an accident. At the same time, it allowed the cars to go faster.

The 1970s were exciting times for Indy racing. More fans than ever before flocked to Indianapolis on Memorial Day weekend. In 1970 the total prize money topped $1 million. It was a fitting sum, as some of Indy racing's greatest drivers were on the track. Foyt, Andretti, and Jones were joined by Mark Donohue, Gordon Johncock, Johnny Rutherford, Al Unser, and Bobby Unser. Each won the Indy 500 at least once during the decade.

In the early 1970s, Indy racing continued to borrow technology from Formula One. Like Formula One cars, Indy cars sprouted wings. With the downforce created by wings, cars were able to top 200 miles (322 km) per hour on the straight parts of the track.

Ground effects were another way to use downforce. Cars with ground effects were part of Indy car designs in 1979. Car builders created tunnels on the underside of the car. Air flows under the car through the tunnels, creating suction. The car is practically glued to the ground. Ground effects made going around corners even quicker. On oval tracks, where cars make one left turn after another, ground effects are the key to speed.

Mark Donohue powers his number 66 McLaren down the Speedway's front straight on his way to winning the 1972 Indy 500. The talented and versatile driver died after a crash in 1975.

By 1979 Indy car racing was extremely popular. The sport was earning a great deal of money for everyone involved. That year, a group of race team owners formed a second sanctioning body. In addition to USAC, which was formed in the 1950s and operated Indy, Championship Auto Racing Teams (CART) was created. Soon CART was in charge of organizing the national championship, called the CART National Championship.

Speeds kept increasing. In 1982 the Indy 500 purse (total prize) hit $2 million. By 1986 it had climbed to $4 million. Rick Mears, Emerson Fittipaldi, Bobby Rahal, and Al Unser Jr. were some of the hottest drivers. Fittipaldi, from Brazil, was one of several Formula One drivers who came to race Indy cars for the big money.

In the late 1980s and early 1990s, speeds began to top 220 miles (354 km) per hour. One reason for this was the use of new materials. Kevlar and carbon fiber replaced metal. Builders used these light and extremely strong materials to build monocoques, wings, and many other parts. The materials made the cars lighter, safer, and quicker. With star drivers, state-of-the-art cars, huge crowds, big purses, and strong television ratings, CART seemed set for a bright future.

New Directions

Then in 1996, the members of CART went in new directions. Indianapolis Motor Speedway owner Tony George—Tony Hulman's grandson—created the Indy Racing League (IRL). George wanted to run a series that offered more opportunities for Americans, especially teams and drivers who were not extremely wealthy. He wanted more races on oval tracks instead of CART's mix of ovals and road courses. His critics said he wanted more money and attention for the big race on his own track, the Indy 500.

Since 1996 the IRL has governed the Indy 500, plus its own series of races. Most of its races take place on oval tracks in the United States. After 1996,

Nigel Mansell of Great Britain in the pits at the Indianapolis Motor Speedway in 1993. The 1992 Formula One World Champion was one of many drivers who came to the United States to race Indy race cars in the 1980s and early 1990s.

On Track

Most IRL car races take place on oval-shaped tracks. The IRL also races on permanent road courses—twisting, turning tracks that are built to challenge drivers with many kinds of turns. Races at Watkins Glen International in New York and Infineon Raceway in California are run on road tracks. Many Champ Car races, such as the Streets of Long Beach race in California, are held on temporary street tracks. City streets are blocked off especially for the race.

many of CART's races were held on road tracks.

The breakup of CART made for some strange Indy 500s in the late 1990s. A number of CART teams chose not to participate in the big race. Some fans argued that the competition was weak. But by 1998, rule changes drew more CART teams back to Indy. The race's tight competition and sense of importance began to return.

But apart from Indy, the two series remained separate, and having two rival series took its toll. Many fans lost interest in the somewhat watered-down competition. CART ran out of money in 2003. A group of team owners saved the series. They renamed it the Champ Car World Series. Since 2004 Champ Car races have been held in the United States, Canada, Mexico, and Australia. Champ Car races took place on oval tracks, permanent road tracks, superspeedways, and temporary road tracks. In 2004 the IRL added some road races to its schedule.

Racing Ahead

IndyCar Series driver Dan Wheldon won the 2005 Indy 500. But rookie Danica Patrick stole the spotlight. Patrick was the first woman to hold the lead in the big race. She finished fourth, becoming the highest-finishing

The talented and likable Danica Patrick brought the IRL a huge dose of star power when she broke into the league in 2005.

woman in Indy 500 history. She also earned Rookie of the Year honors for the season.

The 2006 Indy 500 brought the race's second-closest finish. Sam Hornish Jr. edged out rookie Marco Andretti for the win. The grandson of the great Mario Andretti was followed by his father, Michael, who finished third. A summer of thrilling races followed. Hornish, Wheldon, Scott Dixon, and Helio Castroneves battled down to the last laps of the season to

Ladies and Gentlemen, Start Your Engines

Only four women have raced in the Indy 500. The first was Janet Guthrie *(right)*. She competed from 1977 until 1979. Her best finish was in 1978, when she came in ninth. Lyn St. James competed from 1992 until 1997 and in 2000. Sarah Fisher raced between 2000 and 2004. (She returned to the IRL late in 2006). And in 2005, Danica Patrick took the Indy 500 by storm, finishing fourth in her rookie race.

Sam Hornish Jr. pumps his fist in celebration after beating Marco Andretti to the finish line at the 2006 Indy 500.

decide the IndyCar Series championship. Hornish took the crown in the closest title race in the series' history. Meanwhile, Marco Andretti showed he was a star of the future by winning his first IndyCar Series race, as well as the Rookie of the Year award.

As the Indy 500 comes up to its hundredth birthday, the racing is as exciting as ever. But as the two series continue, fans' loyalties are divided.

Some racing fans have turned to NASCAR stock-car racing. But others remain loyal to Indy-style racing. In 2006 the media reported rumors of a possible Champ Car-IRL unification. But no timetable has been set for bringing the two series together. Whatever the future brings, Indy car racing offers fans a look at high-tech vehicles, thrilling speeds, and spectacular racing excitement.

Tony Kanaan leads the 2006 Watkins Glen Indy Grand Prix in Watkins Glen, New York.

Indy race cars feature ground effects–the underbody of the car is sculpted so as to create a vacuum beneath the car at high speeds. The vacuum sucks the car to the track. In fact, an Indy race car running at 220 miles (354 km) per hour creates so much downforce that it could run upside down (sticking to a ceiling, for example)!

Indy Race Car

Chassis: Carbon fiber and other materials
Constructor: Dallara (Italy) or Panoz (USA)
Engine: 183-cubic inch (3.5-liter) Honda V8
Horsepower: 650+

Length: 192 inches (488 centimeters) min.
Width: 78 in. (198 cm) min.
Weight: 1,525 pounds (692 kilograms) min.
Cost: $309,000

The Champ Car World Series switched to a new car for the 2007 season. The Panoz DP01 is safer, more reliable, and more affordable than the older Lola Champ Car. Like Indy race cars, the Panoz DP01 features ground effects. Its engine is turbocharged. A turbocharger is a device that uses exhaust gases to boost horsepower.

Champ Car

Chassis: Carbon fiber and other materials
Constructor: Panoz (USA)
Engine: 161-ci (2.65 ltr) turbocharged Ford Cosworth V8
Horsepower: 750+

Length: 190 in. (483 cm) min.
Width: 78 in. (198 cm) min.
Weight: 1,460 lbs. (662 kg) min.
Cost: $295,000

Formula One racing is called the "pinnacle (the highest point) of motor sports." For decades, F1 cars have been on the cutting edge of technology. The machines are constructed by the sport's individual teams and are developed throughout the season. For the past several years, F1 has held a grand prix race at the Indianapolis Motor Speedway.

Formula One Race Car

Chassis: Carbon fiber and other materials
Constructor: various
Engine: 146-ci (2.4 ltr) various manufacturers
Horsepower: 700+

Length: 184 in. (467 cm)
Width: 71 in. (180 cm)
Weight: 1,323 lbs. (600 kg) including driver
Cost: varies

The Nextel Cup is the top level of NASCAR competition. Cup cars are loosely based on cars built by major automobile manufacturers–the Chevrolet Monte Carlo, Ford Fusion, Dodge Charger, and Toyota Camry. NASCAR cars are heavier than open-wheel race cars. Their fenders and steel bodywork allow the cars to bump one another at high speed without causing major wrecks.

NASCAR Nextel Cup Stock Car

Chassis: Steel tube frame with steel bodyworks
Constructor: various
Engine: 358-ci (5.8 ltr) V8, various manufacturers
Horsepower: 800+

Length: 199 in. (505 cm)
Width: 72 in. (183 cm)
Weight: 3,400 lbs. (1,542 kg)
Cost: varies

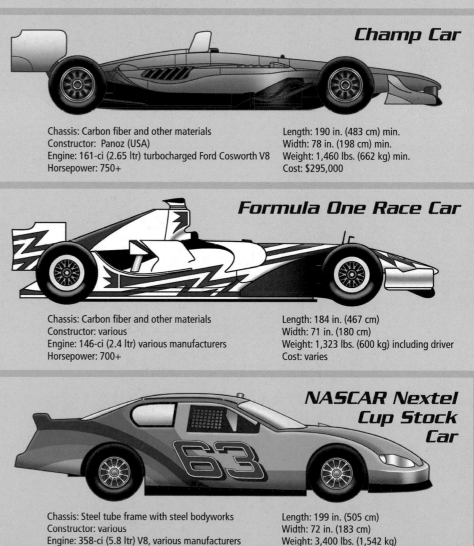

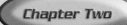

Chapter Two

INDY RACING CULTURE

Dan Wheldon, the 2005 Indy 500 winner, kisses the famous Borg-Warner Trophy, which is presented to the race winner.

The IndyCar Series and Champ Car World Series seasons run from early spring until fall. Drivers and their teams spend the winter getting their cars ready for the upcoming season. And everyone makes an extra-special effort for the Indy 500. They focus on speed, safety, and strategy. They spend millions of dollars searching for the winning combination of parts, settings, and safety features.

Getting Ready

Each driver is part of a team that includes designers, engineers, builders, drivers, and mechanics. The teams are usually run by wealthy racing fans, former race car drivers, or private companies. For example, former race car driver Roger Penske runs Penske Racing. Former driver Bobby Rahal and television-show host David Letterman own Rahal Letterman Racing.

Who Is Roger Penske?

Roger Penske (*right*) is the owner of one of the IRL's top teams. The Penske Racing team has won more races, national championships, and Indy 500s than any other team. Penske also owns a NASCAR® team. A former race car driver, Penske runs businesses ranging from car dealerships to a truck leasing company. Indy 500 winners who have raced for Penske include Mark Donohue; Rick Mears; Emerson Fittipaldi; Helio Castroneves; Sam Hornish Jr. (*left*); Gil de Ferran; and Al Sr., Al Jr., and Bobby Unser.

All teams must use engines, chassis, and tires from the same manufacturers. For example, all IndyCar Series cars use Honda engines and Firestone tires. Chassis are made by Dallara or Panoz. But it's up to the teams to find the best ways to make all the parts work together. The teams test their cars in a factory. They experiment with different parts and settings. Once the

Late-night talk show host and IRL team owner David Letterman watches the 2004 Indy 500.

Indy cars are covered with names and logos of sponsors (*above*). Money from sponsorship deals has helped to fund racing's many technological advances in speed and safety.

car is fit for the track, drivers work with the other team members to test it. The team works together to make improvements to the car.

Running a team is expensive. Building just one car costs more than $400,000. Each team usually has two or more drivers and three or four cars. Other costs include team member salaries, transporting the cars from race to race, and buying replacement parts. Some teams spend up to $10 million each year.

To help with some of the costs, each team has sponsors. The sponsors are companies that pay the teams to advertise for them. Sponsors' names appear on the cars, on team uniforms, and on the trucks that transport the cars from race to race.

Safety

Teams build cars to be fast. But they are also concerned about safety. Serious injuries and even death are always possible. In 2006 IRL driver Paul Dana was killed in an accident. Dana crashed during morning practice for the Toyota Indy 300 at the Homestead-Miami Speedway. He died a few hours later. Because of accidents like this, the IRL is constantly exploring ways to improve safety.

The drivers are strapped tightly into their cars with strong safety harnesses. Their clothing and accessories are designed to survive fires. Drivers wear fireproof suits. Everything else they wear is fireproof—gloves, padded leather shoes, a face mask, and long underwear. Drivers also wear strong helmets made of carbon fiber or fiberglass.

The cars themselves are built of strong, lightweight carbon fiber. When they crash, the cars break apart. With parts flying everywhere, crashes may look scary. But the cars are designed to break. As the parts fly off, they absorb some of the impact of the crash so that the driver isn't hurt.

The Dangers of Open-Wheel Racing

Ryan Briscoe touches wheels with Alex Barron at over 200 miles (322 km) per hour. The contact launches Briscoe into the wall *(right)*.

His car cracks in half *(right)* and bursts into flames.

Rescue workers run to put out the flames. Incredibly, Briscoe suffered no serious injuries. He was well pro-tected inside the car's carbon fiber monocoque *(below)*.

HANS

A crash can cause serious injuries to a driver's head and neck. Helmets and padding in the cockpit can stop some injuries. But a driver's head can still move violently if the car comes to a sudden stop. The Head and Neck Support (HANS) system *(left)* helps to control these violent movements. HANS is a system of a special collar, straps, and a shoulder harness. The system works together to keep the driver's head from whipping around in a crash.

The carbon fiber monocoque is almost indestructible. It protects the driver from even the most violent impacts.

Tracks continue to be updated for improved safety too. Slamming into a track's concrete walls is a common but dangerous kind of accident. But all IRL oval tracks have Steel and Foam Energy Reduction (SAFER) barriers. When the cars hit the walls, the SAFER barrier system absorbs some of the impact. SAFER barriers are made of systems of steel tubes. A layer of foam

This close-up of Tony Kanaan's Indy car clearly shows the slick tires used by the IRL and the Champ Car World Series. More rubber on the road means more traction. Slicks provide the best grip in dry conditions.

sits between the steel tubing and the outer concrete wall.

The Month of May

The month of May is the most exciting time for Indy car racing. Drivers spend much of the month getting ready for the most important race of the year. Teams arrive in Indianapolis on the first weekend of the month. They have several days to practice. Then drivers have four days to qualify for the race.

On each of the qualifying days, cars have three chances to take four laps around the track. The average speed of the four laps is calculated. The driver with the fastest average speed on the first day of time trials gets to start the race in pole position—the inside of the front row. The Indy 500 starts with 11 rows of three cars.

May offers events for Indy fans as well. Fans can watch the qualifying

Teams use semitrailers *(above)* to transport their cars and equipment from track to track.

Sam Hornish Jr. streaks away from the pits during a qualifying session for the Indy 500.

GASOLINE ALLEY

Tony Kanaan's car is pushed through the Speedway's famous garage area, Gasoline Alley.

events. They can check out their favorite drivers and pick out new young guns. They can stroll through the garage area, called Gasoline Alley. Meanwhile, Indianapolis is a giant festival ground, with parades, a foot race, activities for children, and even a ball.

The Race

On the Sunday of Memorial Day weekend, fans cheer wildly as the drivers get ready to race. They hear the magic words, "Ladies and gentlemen, start your engines." Mechanics start up the car engines, and the drivers are off. A

pace car leads the drivers twice around the track to warm up. On the third lap—the pace lap—the pace car sets a controlled speed for the start. Then the race really begins. A starter waves a green flag, the pace car veers off the track, and the racers begin to fight for the lead.

The cars zoom around and around the track. The drivers look for the fastest ways to go around the turns.

Drivers choose when to pass other cars. A driver may pass another on the inside of a turn. A driver may also sneak around another car's right side. One racing technique is drafting. One car gets behind another. The first car blocks the wind for the second car. The lack of air behind the first car creates a vacuum. The first car actually pulls the second car. The second car can use the boost to pass the first car or stay behind and save fuel.

Drivers keep an eye out for accidents or slower cars. They look for flags warning them of danger. And they communicate with their team via radios in their helmets. They get help from people in the pits and spotters. Spotters stand on top of the grandstands watching the race. From there, they are able to suggest the next move or warn their drivers about trouble ahead. Most of all, drivers focus on racing smart and fast.

Cars race in tight packs in order to catch the draft of the cars in front of them.

Part of running a smart race is planning pit stops well. Cars can usually go about 75 miles (120 km) between each pit stop. Then they need to stop to get just the right amount of fuel. Too much fuel makes the car heavy and slow. Racing with little fuel makes the car lighter (and thus, faster). But the car also risks running out of fuel. During a pit stop, the team must judge exactly how much fuel will allow the car to run the best race.

The car pulls into the pits. It slows down and stops in a pit stall. The pit crew—a group of speedy mechanics—gets busy. They refuel the car, change its tires, and make repairs and adjustments. Then the driver is off again. All of this happens in just a few seconds.

More than 300,000 fans cheer during the 2006 Indy 500.

Most pit stops take about 10 seconds, but some are as quick as 7 seconds!

Finishing

After three hours of intense competition, the final laps arrive. Some cars have crashed. Some have dropped out of the race with mechanical problems. The drivers who are still on the track battle for the best position. The white flag comes out. One more lap! Fans jump to their feet. Drivers roar toward the finish. Then the checkered flag waves. The lucky, talented, and happy winner emerges. He might do a few donuts—spinning his car in circles. Or, like two-time Indy 500 winner Helio Castroneves, he might climb a fence out of sheer joy.

The winner moves into Victory Lane to celebrate. He is decked with a wreath of flowers. He takes part in Indy victory traditions such as gulping milk and posing with the giant Borg-Warner Trophy. Indy 500 winners get points toward the IndyCar Series championship. But most importantly, the winner gets to join a small group of Indy 500 champions. His—or someday her—name will shine forever as an Indy racing legend.

TRACKS

Open-wheel race cars compete on a variety of different kinds of racetracks. Most IRL races take place on ovals of different sizes and shapes. In recent seasons, the series has added some permanent road courses to its schedule. On the other hand, nearly all Champ Car World Series races take place on either permanent road courses or on temporary street circuits. Street courses are regular city streets that are closed off from traffic for the events. Below is a selection of different IRL and Champ Car courses. To the right is a map showing the locations of these tracks.

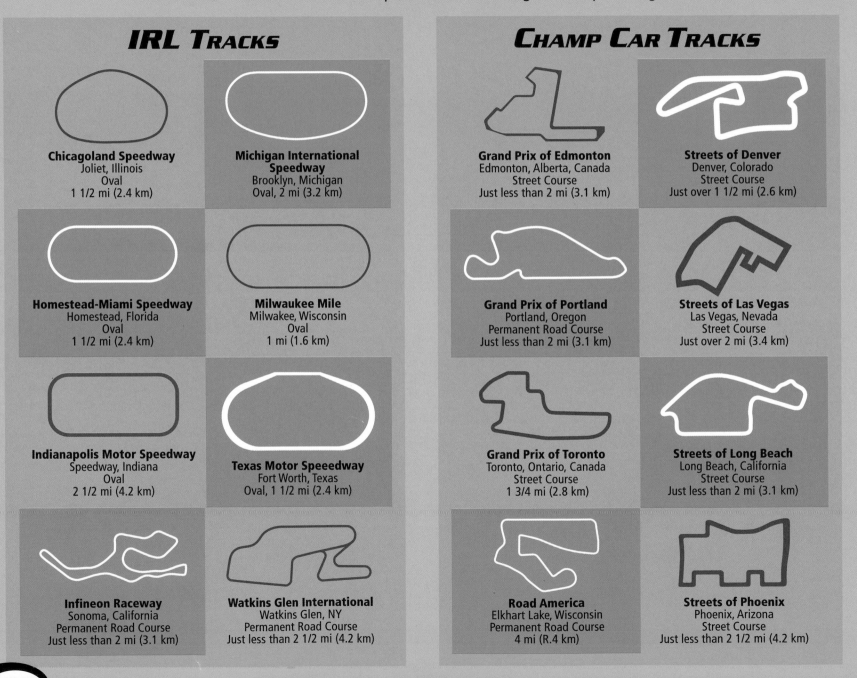

IRL TRACKS

Chicagoland Speedway
Joliet, Illinois
Oval
1 1/2 mi (2.4 km)

Michigan International Speedway
Brooklyn, Michigan
Oval, 2 mi (3.2 km)

Homestead-Miami Speedway
Homestead, Florida
Oval
1 1/2 mi (2.4 km)

Milwaukee Mile
Milwakee, Wisconsin
Oval
1 mi (1.6 km)

Indianapolis Motor Speedway
Speedway, Indiana
Oval
2 1/2 mi (4.2 km)

Texas Motor Speeedway
Fort Worth, Texas
Oval, 1 1/2 mi (2.4 km)

Infineon Raceway
Sonoma, California
Permanent Road Course
Just less than 2 mi (3.1 km)

Watkins Glen International
Watkins Glen, NY
Permanent Road Course
Just less than 2 1/2 mi (4.2 km)

CHAMP CAR TRACKS

Grand Prix of Edmonton
Edmonton, Alberta, Canada
Street Course
Just less than 2 mi (3.1 km)

Streets of Denver
Denver, Colorado
Street Course
Just over 1 1/2 mi (2.6 km)

Grand Prix of Portland
Portland, Oregon
Permanent Road Course
Just less than 2 mi (3.1 km)

Streets of Las Vegas
Las Vegas, Nevada
Street Course
Just over 2 mi (3.4 km)

Grand Prix of Toronto
Toronto, Ontario, Canada
Street Course
1 3/4 mi (2.8 km)

Streets of Long Beach
Long Beach, California
Street Course
Just less than 2 mi (3.1 km)

Road America
Elkhart Lake, Wisconsin
Permanent Road Course
4 mi (R.4 km)

Streets of Phoenix
Phoenix, Arizona
Street Course
Just less than 2 1/2 mi (4.2 km)

Alberta

CANADA

Grand Prix of Edmonton

Ontario

Michigan International Speedway

Grand Prix of Portland

Grand Prix of Toronto

OR

WI

Road America

Milwaukee Mile

MI

NY

Infineon Raceway

NV

Watkins Glen International

Streets of Las Vegas

Streets of Denver

Chicagoland Speedway

IN

CA

CO

Indianapolis Motor Speedway

Streets of Long Beach

AZ

IL

UNITED STATES

Streets of Phoenix

Texas Motor Speedway

MEXICO

TX

FL

Homestead-Miami Speedway

Mario Andretti (born 1940)

This Italian-born American is one of the best all-around drivers ever. Andretti excelled in Indy racing, as well as Formula One racing, stock-car racing, and other events. Andretti is the only person to have won the Indy 500, the Formula One World Championship, and the Daytona 500.

Seasons: 1965–1978, 1980–1994

Wins: 52

Indianapolis 500 Wins: 1

Series Championships: 4

Michael Andretti (born 1962)

The son of Mario, Michael has raced in Formula One, the IRL, and CART. Although he never won the Indy 500, Michael is one of the top Indy car drivers ever. Only his father and A. J. Foyt have won more races. Michael owns Andretti Green Racing, one of the top IRL teams, and his son Marco joined the IndyCar Series in 2006. Michael made a comeback at Indy in 2006, finishing third.

Seasons: 1983–1992, 1994–2003, 2006*

Wins: 42

Indianapolis 500 Wins: 0

Series Championships: 1

*Competed in Indy 500 only

Mario Andretti, 1975

Michael Andretti, 2002

Helio Castroneves (born 1975)

This intense and fun-loving Brazilian is one of the IRL's biggest stars. He has earned the nickname "Spiderman" because he celebrates his race wins by climbing a fence to get close to the fans. A two-time Indy 500 winner, Castroneves battled his Penske teammate Sam Hornish Jr. down to the wire for the 2006 IndyCar Series Championship.

Seasons: 1998–

Wins: 11

Indianapolis 500 wins: 2

Series Championships: 0

Ralph DePalma (1884–1956)

One of racing's early stars, DePalma was known for his good sportsmanship. He continued to race after retiring from Indy racing. DePalma claimed to have won more than 2,500 races in his career.

Seasons: 1911–1913, 1915, 1919–1923, 1925

Wins: 25

Indianapolis 500 Wins: 1

Series Championships: 2

Helio Castroneves, 2006

Ralph DePalma, 1915

A. J. Foyt (born 1935)

This tough Texan is one of the most successful race car drivers ever. Super Tex was the first driver to win the Indy 500 four times. He also competed in other kinds of racing, winning the Daytona 500 and the 24 Hours of Le Mans. He competed 35 times in a row in the Indy 500. Foyt remains active in the IRL as a team owner.

Seasons: 1958–1992

Wins: 67

Indianapolis 500 Wins: 4

Series Championships: 7

Sam Hornish Jr. (born 1979)

The Ohio native is considered one of the IndyCar Series' best oval racers. In 2006 the Penske Racing driver finally achieved his childhood dream by winning the Indy 500. He finished his stellar 2006 season by winning the IndyCar Series championship in one of the closest title fights ever.

Seasons: 2000–

Wins: 18

Indianapolis 500 Wins: 1

Series Championships: 3

A. J. Foyt, 1973

Sam Hornish Jr., 2006

Rick Mears (born 1951)

Known for his intense focus and drive to win, Mears was the youngest person to win the Indy 500 four times. Mears raced for Roger Penske's team. Since Mears's retirement, he has worked as a consultant for the team. His nephew Casey Mears races in NASCAR.

Seasons: 1978–1992

Wins: 29

Indianapolis 500 Wins: 4

Series Championships: 3

Louis Meyer (1904–1995)

Meyer was not just the first Indy 500 winner to drink milk in Victory Lane—he was also the first driver to win the race three times. After retiring as a driver, Meyer worked to develop racing engines.

Seasons: 1928–1939

Wins: 8

Indianapolis 500 Wins: 3

Series Championships: 3

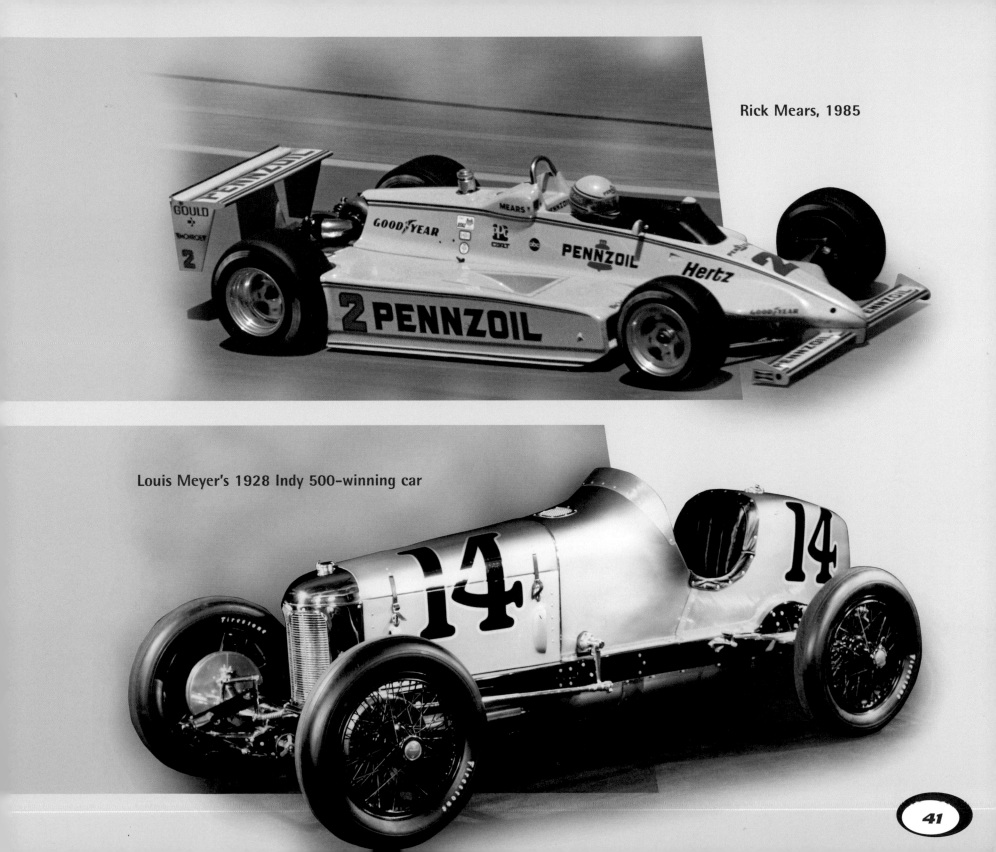

Rick Mears, 1985

Louis Meyer's 1928 Indy 500-winning car

Wilbur Shaw (1902–1954)

The three-time Indy 500 winner was a pioneer in racing safety. He began wearing a crash helmet in 1932. After his retirement from racing, Shaw served as the president of the Indianapolis Motor Speedway, helping to save it from ruin after World War II.

Seasons: 1927–28, 1930, 1932–1941

Wins: 6

Indianapolis 500 Wins: 3

Series Championships: 2

Al Unser Jr. (born 1962)

"Little Al" is the son of Al Unser Sr. and the nephew of Bobby Unser. He grew up surrounded by racing and followed in his family's footsteps to many victories. He raced for both CART and the IRL. Al Jr. retired in 2004 but came back to race at Indy in 2006.

Seasons: 1982–2004, 2006*

Wins: 34

Indianapolis 500 Wins: 2

Series Championships: 2

*Competed in Indy 500 only

Wilbur Shaw, 1940

Al Unser Jr., 1991

Al Unser Sr. (born 1939)

A member of one of racing's most successful families, Al Sr. shares the honor of having won the Indy 500 with his brother Bobby and son Al Jr. But Al Sr. has won it more than any other Unser—four times. He is one of only three drivers to achieve the feat.

Seasons: 1965–1990, 1992–1993

Wins: 39

Indianapolis 500 Wins: 4

Series Championships: 3

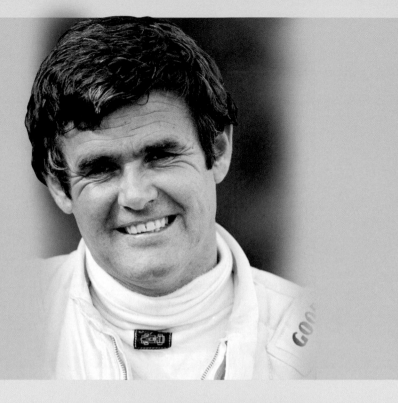

Bobby Unser (born 1934)

In 1968, Bobby became the first Unser to win the Indy 500. He went on to win the big race two more times, in 1975 and 1981. Bobby was the first driver to hit 190 miles (306 km) per hour at Indy. He is also known for competing in the Pike's Peak Hill Climb.

Seasons: 1963–1981

Wins: 35

Indianapolis 500 Wins: 3

Series Championships: 2

Al Unser Sr., 1987

Bobby Unser, 1975

Glossary

aerodynamic: shaped so that air flows smoothly over and around an object

bodywork: the outside of a car. It covers the engine and other mechanical parts.

chassis: the main part of an Indy car. The other parts of the car are attached to the chassis.

downforce: air pushing down on a car as it moves forward

drafting: a racing strategy in which one car closely follows another. The first car blocks the airflow on the second car, creating a vacuum. The first car tows the second car.

ground effects: tunnels on the underside of a car that create downforce

monocoque: a narrow tube-shaped section that makes up part of the main part of an Indy car. The cockpit is in the monocoque.

open wheel: a kind of race car that has no fenders on the wheels

pits: an area next to the track where drivers can stop during a race to make repairs, refuel, and change tires

pole position: the inside spot in the front row of cars in the starting lineup. The car that qualifies for the race with the fastest time gets to start here.

sponsors: companies that provide financial support for racing teams. Sponsors pay teams to advertise for them.

suspension: the parts that connect the wheels to the main part of the car

Selected Bibliography

Hobbs, David. Telephone interview by author. Madison, WI, October 20, 2005.

Indianapolis 500. 2005. http://www.indy500.com/ (November 26, 2005).

IndyCar Series. 2005. http://www.indycar.com/home.php (November 26, 2005).

Mauk, Erik. E-mail interview by author. Madison, WI, October 31, 2005.

Rendall, Ivan. *The Power and the Glory: A Century of Motor Racing*. London: BBC Books, 1991.

Sakkis, Tony. *Indy Racing Legends*. Osceola, WI: Motorbooks International Publishers & Wholesalers, 1996.

Taylor, Rich. *Indy: Seventy-Five Years of Racing's Greatest Spectacle*. New York: St. Martin's Press, 1991.

Pimm, Nancy Roe. *Indy 500: The Inside Track*. Plain City, OH: Darby Creek Publishing, 2004.

Raby, Philip. *Racing Cars*. Minneapolis: LernerSports, 1999.

Savage, Jeff. *Danica Patrick*. Minneapolis: Lerner Publications Company, 2007.

Further Reading

Doeden, Matt. *Stock Cars*. Minneapolis: Lerner Publications Company, 2007.

Piehl, Janet. *Formula One Race Cars*. Minneapolis: Lerner Publications Company, 2007.

Websites

Champ Car World Series
http://www.champcarworldseries.com
Champ Car's fact-packed site offers race schedules, news, and helpful background information about the racing series.

Indianapolis 500
http://www.indy500.com/
The website of the Indianapolis 500 provides information about the big race, plus statistics about past races and historical and fun facts.

IndyCar Series
http://www.indycar.com/home.php
The Indy Racing League's site features news and information about the most current races, plus information about cars and drivers.

Index

Andretti, Marco, 6, 9, 26, 34

Andretti, Mario, 13, 14, 19, 34, 35

Andretti, Michael, 19, 34, 35

Andretti Green Racing, 6, 34

Borg-Warner Trophy, 22, 31

CART-IRL split, 17, 18, 20

Castroneves, Helio, 19, 23, 31, 36, 37

Champ Car World Series, 4, 18, 20, 21, 26, 36

Championship Auto Racing Teams (CART), 16, 17, 18

DePalma, Ralph, 36, 37

Donohue, Mark, 15, 23

Duesenberg, 9

Fisher, Carl, 8

Formula One cars, 15, 21

Foyt, A. J., 13, 15, 38, 39

George, Tony, 17

Guthrie, Janet, 19

Harroun, Ray, 9

Hornish, Sam, Jr., 19, 23, 27, 30, 31, 38, 39

Hulman, Anton (Tony), 11, 17

Indianapolis Motor Speedway: origins of, 8; safety improvements made to, 10, 11, 26

Indy cars: capabilities of, 4, 8, 9, 11, 12, 15, 16; characteristics of, 4, 6, 7, 9, 12, 13, 14, 15, 16; development of, 9, 11, 12, 13, 14, 15, 16; safety of, 14, 16, 24, 25, 26

IndyCar Series, 4, 23, 34, 38

Indy 500: average speeds achieved during, 4, 8, 9, 11, 12, 15, 16; events surrounding, 4, 23, 27, 28, 31; fatalities at, 10, 12; traditions of, 4, 22, 28, 31

Indy Racing League (IRL), 4, 17, 18, 19, 20, 22, 24, 26, 31

Kanaan, Tony, 26, 28

Kurtis, Frank, 12

Letterman, David, 22, 23

Mears, Rick, 16, 23, 40, 41

Meyer, Louis, 40, 41

monocoque, 6, 14, 25

Patrick, Danica, 18, 19

Penske, Roger, 22, 23, 40

Rahal Letterman Racing, 22

Rickenbacker, Eddie, 10

Rutherford, Johnny, 16

Shaw, Wilbur, 42, 43

Speedway, Indiana, 4

sponsors, 24

stock cars, 21

Unser, Al, Jr., 16, 23, 42, 43

Unser, Al, Sr., 15, 23, 44, 45

Unser, Bobby, 15, 23, 44, 45

Vukovich, Bill, 12

Wheldon, Dan, 7, 18, 22

About the Author

Janet Piehl is a children's librarian and writer. A former children's book editor, she is also the author of two books about Formula One racing. She lives in Wisconsin.

About the Consultant

Jan Lahtonen is a safety engineer and auto mechanic. He has raced sports cars and worked as a performance driving instructor. He has followed car racing for more than 40 years.

Photo Acknowledgments